Knowings

Knowings

a journey to contentment
through the heart's window

mary backlund

maxzamum press

Published by maxzamum press
www.artandsoulbymaryb.com

07 06 05 04 03 ~ 5 4 3 2 1

PUBLISHER CATALOGING-IN-PUBLICATION DATA
Backlund, Mary
Knowings : a journey to contentment through the
heart's window / mary b
p.   cm.
ISBN 0-9742279-0-0
Library of Congress Number: 2003107999
[1. Self-perception. 2. Awareness. 3. Mental healing.
4. Mind and body. 5. Contentment] I. Title.
BF697.5.S43 B33 2003
158.1—dc21   CIP

Printed in the United States of America

Project coordinated by To The Point Solutions
www.tothepointsolutions.com

COVER & ILLUSTRATIONS: Mary Backlund
TEXT DESIGN: Mary Jo Zazueta, To The Point Solutions

To Jim
thank you for showing me what
hearts are meant for and that
anything is possible.
You are what dreams are made of.

To Max and Zach
for keeping my heart open with laughter.

Contents

Preface

A gathering of inspirations that can be read and lived daily—more than once—over and over.

Read them. Breathe them. Feel them. Affirm them. Let them lead you to the truth within your self. Your world will brighten because your true light will shine.

My vision is that you will carry this book with you, in your heart and in your backpack. Let these thoughts and words become a part of you.

Namaste*

*Hindu: From the god/good in me to the god/good in you. Peace and love.

Special Thanks to:

Tricia, for giving me answers before I knew there were questions.

Sandy, for spilling the paint with me.

Mom, for believing in me, always, always. And for letting me stay up late writing & pretending not to see my flashlight!

Mary Jo, you made it comfortable and REAL!

Sandra, for showing me the stars, the path.

Sacred Circle, my dear ones, you are magic. I thank you & love you!

Knowings

Introduction

Why read Knowings?

You have only one mission: To make your soul content. Only then are you true to your self and whole. This is when you are of the greatest good to your self and those you love.

We tend to focus on the well-being of others. But when YOU are full, wholesome, and content the world is better because of it.

Think of how you feel when a dear friend is happy after a bout of disconnectedness. Think of how you feel when your spouse is loving. Think of the utter joy you relish when your child has recovered from an injury to the heart. That is how the gods celebrate your wholeness ~ your contentedness.

k n o w i n g s

I am content. I am honoring the voice in me that says, "Take time." I am celebrating me.

get a grip by letting go

While taking an early morning walk with a dear girlfriend, we contemplated the "virtue" of hanging on to our pains (broken hearts, mothers, fathers, self-doubt, etc.). I suddenly realized I was hanging on to this familiar, uncomfortable, need-to-be-in-control feeling because if I let go, I wasn't sure what I would think, feel, or DO.

Then I knew the answer: I could DO whatever I wanted! Because I was free.

Letting Go means freedom. Letting Go gives us permission to be happy and to move on. Letting Go honors the hurt and the event and allows us to fill up with light.

k n o w i n g s

Letting Go makes room for "now!" For the good, the love, the joys and opportunities that can only be experienced when you take off the blinders of "hanging on."

Letting Go gives your heart room to sing and to grow wings of faith. Faith in yourself.

I am letting go of negative thoughts. I am filling myself up with joyful thoughts. I am free!

9

when your light is on, life is easier and simpler

What is it like when your light is on? You walk on air. Your breathing is full and calm. You have patience at a red light. The nosy neighbor doesn't bother you.

What does it feel like when your light is on? Remember the first time you fell in love? Remember the joy of getting the job you really wanted? Remember the satisfaction of cooking a great meal? Remember the contentment of completing an arduous task?

How do you keep your light on? You find the blessings in each day; not just at night before bed, but throughout the day. You say "thank you" often. You take time for yourself every single day. You rediscover play (what makes

your spirit sing?). You let go of past
expectations and rediscover yourself. And then,
you rest. And let the goodness fill you up.

knowings

My light is on. I am breathing
fully and peacefully. I am thankful
for _____.

Thank You!

living well is the best tonic

According to Merriam-Webster's Dictionary, "tonic" is something that invigorates, restores, or refreshes.

Living well includes the following:

- Large doses of love. Let yourself be loved daily, by others and yourself. Giving your self time each day to do something that excites you and fills you up (i.e., playing the piano, doing yoga, painting your front door a beautiful blue, photographing the red maple that exploded in color overnight, or listening to your favorite music).

- Go to bed. You need so much more rest than you allow your self. If you're not

knowings

used to this ~ go to bed anyhow! Have
you forgotten all the fun things you used
to do in bed? Read. Look at old
photographs. Write a letter. Daydream.
Journal. Make love.

- Renew the connection with the god of
  your comfort level. You've never had one?
  Spirit is waiting for you. Just ask. Listen.
  You will be answered.

I am finding comfort daily. I am laughing. I am resting. I am living whole and well. The god in me is connecting with the god of my choice.

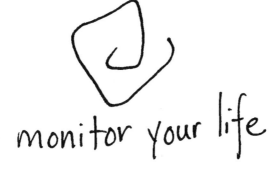

monitor your life

What do you want? What do you need for your spirit to be content (the red leather pumps in the catalogue don't count)? Do you want to be less busy? OK, then ~ go to your calendar and delete one commitment for this month (I dare you to delete two). Come on ~ make the phone call. There! Do you feel relief? Do you have a strange feeling in your gut? It's pride (you did it!) and joy.

You've begun to live with intention; to put your energy (attention) in a place that builds toward contentment. You are honoring the divine in you, giving it time to breathe and grow.

Some people say their children keep them

busy. Set an example for your children. Tell them you are taking time (say, Wednesday evening) to care for your self. I will sometimes say, "I need some alone time." These are simple words to remember but are often difficult to speak. Practice on someone close to you.

I practiced on my eight-year-old son. He was engaged in his activities and I told him I needed some alone time in the studio. I set the timer for thirty minutes. He could check the timer if he needed to, but I assured him I would be down when it rang.

I am an awesome mom when I come down those stairs thirty minutes later! Don't worry ~ you will come down those stairs. You will return to mothering. And you will be better; mentally and physically. And ~ you will make

knowings

a habit of taking time for your self because people tend to repeat activities that feel good. Your biology will react positively to "contentment-inducing behavior." There will be a peace that will grow within you. It is a necessity for your wholeness and a gift for those around you.

Do you know how often you use and hear the word _stress_ each day? When you hear this word your whole being focuses on ~ STRESS. Just think if you focused on increasing your calmness ~ finding peace in each day. That's what you need to do, see, and hear.

Living with intention also means you monitor the quality of your spirit life. Engage in thoughts and activities that bring you to a contented place. Contentment is not boring or without excitement. Contentment is passion fulfilled. It is vitality. It stays with you, becomes a part of your being. You have it within you now. Take the time to unwrap it. Contentment is divine. The gods smile when you are content.

I am monitoring my life. I am saying yes to the activities that bring me joy. I am honoring my self. I am nourishing my spirit. I am discovering contentment daily.

heart wholeness

Your heart is your altar. Keep it full and well lit.

May you know the feeling of heart wholeness. Truly your mind is only here to balance the checkbook and set the alarm clock. Your heart can and must rule the rest of your whole, wondrous, and full life. Why?

Love is all that matters. Love will rise above all else. It will toast better bread. It will raise healthy, happy children. It will make way for passionate marriages. It will find you the vocation of your dreams. It will bring you home ~ it will bring you to your self.

Only engage in activities that you can bring love to. You must be genuine in what you do.

knowings

By being true to your heart you are honoring that responsibility in others also.

How do you bring this love to fruition? Love your self first. Let go of past expectations and write new rules for your self. Take fifteen minutes each day to think about how you love, are loved, and how it feels. You must feel the energy of love before you can make it a part of your nature and daily doings.

Grab a piece of paper and write down five things that you love about you. Experience that feeling of love in your gut . . . come on . . . remember the time you first fell in love? That's what I'm talking about! Take this time to fall in love with your self. You are unable to love others fully if you don't love your self first. The gods want you to be comfortable with your self. Honor this.

knowings

I am thankful that I have time to learn about my self. I am learning to love and nurture my self. I am living with a whole heart that leads me through my days.

solitude

Solitude is not a four-letter word. The knowings you desire come in times of solitude. The gods visit you then. They nurture you with insight and, sometimes, surprising sites, when you choose your solitude in nature. You must make regular appointments with solitude. Your Franklin Planner will accept this appointment when you write it in.

Solitude is quiet time. It is always done alone and usually without any physical movement. It may be sitting on your porch in your favorite wicker rocker for fifteen uninterrupted minutes (an hour is ideal) looking at your surroundings, journaling, or daydreaming.

Sometimes I get in my van and drive to the

lake. I park facing a serene view and simply allow my mind to settle . . . ponder. I often stay in the van. Sometimes I play music, but I have become comfortable with silence and find myself craving it.

Solitude: simple, sacred, necessary, life-giving. Solitude gives your spirit space and time to reacquaint itself with your being ~ time to fill up your vessel.

I give my self permission to practice solitude. I am using solitude to learn to love my self again by pure reacquaintance. I am filling up my vessel.

gratitude

"Thank you" is the only true prayer.
~ Meister Eckhart

How many times do you remember your
mother or father saying to you, "Be happy
with what you have"? How often did you
respond by thinking, "Yes, but if only I had
. . ."? You must learn the power of gratitude.

Acknowledging your gratitude opens you up to
unrivaled abundance. Finding the pleasures in
each day helps you focus on joy, love, laughter,
and passion—the pure blessings in your
charmed life.

Gratitude draws your attention to the graces
of your blessed life. Thus, you find yourself

knowings

placing your intentions on finding more ~
building from the riches you are discovering
you already have.

Every good teacher knows success builds
success. It is the same with gratitude. The
more you are thankful for, the more you will
find to be thankful for.

When you replace your current sense of lack
with the newfound knowledge of your wealth
and fullness, you will attract more. Gratitude
equals abundance.

As you become aware and fill your vessel with
this precious commodity, beware! You will
become increasingly content. And ~ here's the
big warning ~ be open for the possibilities
that will present themselves to you. Whatever
you wish will be yours, because you will have
the tools to carry it out: noticing details,

knowings

finding joy, knowing your passions, and saying thank you.

Most importantly, you will empower the spirit in you that the gods have been waiting for and placed in you. The power of creation. Creation of your dreams.

knowings

I am finding gratitude in each day.
I am discovering the abundance
that is in my life. I am living my
dreams.

contentment

Contentment is the only goal you need. Let your dreams be for this. Picture your self doing what brings you serenity and joy: painting, running your own business, building your dream house, spending more time at home or with your loved ones, simplifying your life, traveling, or running a marathon.

Know this: contentment comes from within. It does not come from things or other people. You must first be whole with your self to touch this precious jewel.

Contentment begins by putting your attention toward the good, the positive, the laughter in your days, and the charms that dangle on your daily doings.

knowings

Contentment can only be found NOW. Not tomorrow. Not yesterday. Not on a trip last summer. Not when you make "x" amount of money. Not when you have that baby. NOW!

Contentment lies within you. It is similar to enlightenment. The gods give it to you, just as they give you the power to create, to solve problems, to cry, to dance. You already know this. I tell you no secret. I tell you only what I have discovered within my self.

Contentment is "childish" because we are born with it. We seem to grow out of it—like our first pair of shoes ~ and then we forget how to replace it through such natural means as solitude, gratitude, rest, and play.

Remember the first time you held a baby and felt the magic of its peace. That is contentment.

knowings

Contentment is equal doses of faith ~ faith in YOUR sacredness ~ and gratitude ~ for the wholeness you are discovering daily through your positive intentions.

knowings

I am content. I am discovering "peaces" of my life that fill me. I give power to my joy in them. I am breathing contentment into my heart.

synchronicity

Pay attention to the synchronicity in your life. It is the gods talking out loud (sometimes I think they are "pulling my chain"). They want to tell you they are here for you. They are listening to your thoughts and wishes. They are giving you food for thought. They are proving to you that they want to be heard. They want to help. They are within touching and hearing distance. They love you. It is one of their gifts to you.

We've all had glimpses of the divine. Allow me to share some: I needed to get an important message to a friend and my phone was down. She did not live within a comfortable walking distance. She showed up at my doorstep on her way to work to drop off some cookies. This was

not usual behavior for her. I thanked the gods
for their efficiency.

~ ~ ~

I mentioned to my mom, who lives about
three hours away, that I'd really like to take
a watercolor painting class, but I wasn't able
to find one locally that fit into my schedule
and budget. A week later she phoned. An
incredible artist was offering a daylong class
and the cost was $15! I was able to visit home
and spend an entire Saturday learning the art
of watercolor painting. Thank you gods for
leading me to my dreams.

~ ~ ~

I was missing a dear pal but, due to my
budget at the time, I simply couldn't afford
the long-distance phone call. We rarely talked,

but when we did, we spoke our deepest truths.
She phoned that day! She said was thinking
about me. Thank you gods for hearing my
sorrow.

~ ~ ~

Synchronicity happens every day. It's when
your loved one reaches for you just as you
think his name. It's when your son walks
through the door after his first driving
experience on snowy roads. It's when the
potatoes and pork chops finish cooking just as
the boys walk in from soccer practice
announcing their starvation.

It is divine communication. Pay attention.

knowings

I am noticing the synchronicity in my daily doings. I am listening for the gods' answers to my dilemmas. I realize the more I pay attention the more the magic surfaces. I am thankful for my growing awareness.

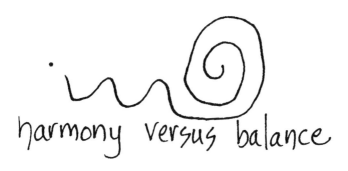

harmony versus balance

Harmony comes from within. Balance is what the world tries to convince you is necessary. Let me explain. Harmony is the flow of enlightenment and daily living. It is the act of allowing your self to trust that what you are doing right now is the most important act. Harmony is a continual stream that lingers with you. It carries you from one action and intention to another. Harmony flows.

Balance, on the other hand, is the act of doing separate things. Trying to give just the right amount (often the same amount) to each event.

Balance is putting things in a line so as not

to upset the cart or show any zigzagging.
Balance is kept on a plate, or worse yet, a
tightrope.

Harmony is not kept anywhere. Rather it is
felt, lived, and most importantly, shared.
Harmony is music. Soul music. Harmony is
when enlightenment and daily living conspire
to make wonderful melodies. Harmony is the
act of allowing your passions (the love of your
family, exercise, a job well done, solitude,
lust, laughter) to coexist.

"This is not possible!" you shout at this page.
You are wrong, dear one ~ the gods created
you with just this in mind. It is their plan.
It is you who limits your life to a balanced
plate or insists on walking a tightrope on a
deadly balance. Instead, allow harmony to flow
through you. The first step to understanding
and living in harmony is to realize you can.

knowings

Harmony tells you that to <u>have</u> it all you don't need to <u>do</u> it all. To have it all is to go within your self. Find the wholeness that resides in you. Begin by checking out your daily doings with your heart and your gut. Ask your self, "How does this feel? Does it feel comfortable?" Then listen to your body. Do you have a knot in your gut? Yes. Is it excitement? Yes. Then go for it! Is it dread (or what I call "icky")? Don't do it.

Your body is with you for the duration of this earthly adventure. It is your constant vessel. Listen to it. Follow its directions. (A good reason to keep your body well fed and exercised.) If you do nothing else ~ follow your heart and gut. Why do you think there are such rampant physical maladies, such as high blood pressure, gall bladder and irritable bowel upsets? People are playing "Follow the

Leader" instead of following their heart's desire, their passions, and their knowings.

Strive for harmony and you will be strengthened by the rejoicing of your inner being ~ the divine ~ the universe. You will feel whole. You will feel true to your self. You will have music in your soul. Your heart will sing.

Today I will look within my self to find the ingredients of my soul music. I will listen to the pieces that make up my harmony. I will do less and have more. I will look to nature to help me find the music that is sometimes difficult to hear in my loud and often busy life. I am doing what feels right for me.

grace

Grace is always with you. It waits patiently for you to ask it to walk beside you or even to lead you at times. Grace wants to show you the magic and contentment you can create with its power.

Grace is divinity. Grace is permission. Grace is your ticket to reach your greatest potential. Ask grace to come forward. Then wait, just a bit. Now, do what it is you want to do. Grace is the lift. Grace is the warm hand on your back. Grace is the peace you receive when you know what is right for you.

Grace is quiet and discreet. It requires a part of you to be still long enough so that you can focus on the task at hand. Grace shows you

how to honor your self by pulling up the
divine energies within you. Grace is a
messenger from the gods ~ a constant
companion and true caretaker, for it allows
you to empower your self, when you need it.

Grace requires belief; belief that you can have
or do something ~ belief that with inner
strength (grace) you can do whatever you need
to at this moment.

Grace is merely an extension of the divinity
that is you. When you realize this, your
dreams, truth, and contentment become real.
And you are whole.

Grace will walk with me and share my heart today and always. I invite Grace to join me on my journey into wholeness. I ask now and always. I experience the grace in my life. I will be still and listen so that I can feel its calm and empowering strength.

faith versus trust

Learn to have faith in your self. Trust can be superficial and a quick fix.

You need to believe that you can thrive in circumstances that are less than desirable.

Knowing there are no mistakes on your journey, faith allows you to delete worry from your emotional word bank.

Take the time and energy to look inward and you will reap knowledge and peace. Have faith in your strength.

Ask for Grace to help you get started.

Trust can mask your potential for incredible, liberating faith. Your soul wants you to be faith-full:

> Full of spirit.
>
> Full of belief.
>
> Full.
>
> Content.

Trust is a human condition. Faith is divine. Choose divinity.

Trust is energy for someone or something else. Trust is attachment, often unfair to all concerned.

You give trust away, but keep it tethered to your heart, pulling ever so often.

Faith is all yours. You own it. It feeds you.
Faith keeps your light on.

Your heart vibrates with enlightenment when
Faith resides there. And think about this: We
speak of "building" trust ~ that sounds like
work. We "have" Faith ~ that sounds natural
. . . simple . . . comfortable.

knowings

I believe I am able to be with my self in any circumstance. I live in Faith. I realize the divinity that resides in me. I envision my heart full of Faith. It glows. I shine.

truth

Your soul has transported the truth into your
heart, because your heart is the best vessel to
carry such a treasure.

Find your truth.

Feel your truth.

Walk your truth.

Be sincere and whole.

"What is your truth? How will you find it?"
IT will discover you! Truth is the tonic, a bit
sour tasting at times, that will let you know
if you're on the path that will lead you to
enlightenment and wholeness.

Truth does not sneak up on you. It looks you
directly in the eye and doesn't blink until you

knowings

speak to it. Truth watches you cry. It feels you ache. It listens as you scream questions at the universe. It knows that only you can answer them ~ that the answers reside in you.

Truth knows you have to do the soul work and wait.

What does truth look like? It is a request from someone that you can't fulfill because it doesn't feel comfortable. So, you say no, even if your answer may cause them discomfort.

Truth is leaving a job that pays well and offers future security so that you can write the book on gardens that's been growing in your mind.

Truth is speaking heartfelt words to a dear one and having them shut you down. And yet, you know, you believe, that you couldn't have done it any other way.

k n o w i n g s

Truth is when you look in the mirror and see the face of a warrior . . . a warrior of the soul that wears the expression of vulnerability and truth. It is not always pretty, but it is always authentic.

Truth is the voice that tells you what you feel and encourages you to do what you feel. Truth is the fuel on the voyage to your self.

I am listening to my heart.
I am finding my truth.

The Author and Artist

Known as mary b., Mary Backlund loves to laugh, paint, sleep, write, and eat ripe strawberries.

She has a master's degree in education and taught all ages for eighteen years.

In 2002, mary b. resigned from teaching to pursue her dreams of art and writing. "Dreams do come true," she sings.

Mary b. spends her days painting decoratively in peoples' homes, writing, and offering classes and workshops on Soul Comfort and the Artist Way (Julia Cameron).

She resides in beautiful northern Michigan with her two sons, Zach and Max, who call her Mom; and her husband of many years, Jim, who calls her Sweetie Pie (most of the time).

For more information on mary b. please visit her colorful and inspiring Web site:
www.artandsoulbymaryb.com

I wish you contentment
and joy !

mb

Published by maxzamum press
www.artandsoulbymaryb.com